Original title:
Life's Puzzle—Where's the Corner Piece?

Copyright © 2025 Creative Arts Management OÜ
All rights reserved.

Author: Victor Mercer
ISBN HARDBACK: 978-1-80566-187-0
ISBN PAPERBACK: 978-1-80566-482-6

Chasing Shadows

I ran after my friend's tall shadow,
But stepped on a dog and tripped on a meadow.
We laughed like fools under the hot sun,
Chasing shadows is way more fun!

We spun around like tops on the ground,
Searching for laughter where it can be found.
But shadows play tricks and dance out of sight,
Just when you think you're catching them right!

Assembling the Unknown

I brought home a box of jumbled pieces,
Thinking I could build a chair for my nieces.
But all I got was a weird-looking throne,
For a king who's better off all alone!

I tried to fit squares in the roundest hole,
And ended up with a coffee cup goal.
Next time I need instructions, clear as day,
Or I'll end up sitting on it anyway!

Incomplete Symphony

My guitar strings broke while I strummed a tune,
And out came a sound that made cows swoon.
A goat joined in with a loud honk and bleat,
I'd call it music, though it missed a beat!

The piano keys still have lots of dust,
Just like my dreams that fade with each gust.
So we dance in circles, arms open wide,
To a symphony only we can decide!

The Unfolding Tapestry

I bought a rug that looked so unique,
But it unraveled and made me freak.
With threads flying wild, chaos in the air,
My cat's now a wizard, but I don't care!

I tried to stitch it back, thought I might learn,
But turned it to confetti; oh, how it did turn!
Now it decorates my floor with flair,
A masterpiece only clumsy hands could bear!

Threads of a Frayed Tapestry

In the fabric of days, threads twist and twine,
Stitching chaos and laughter, it's all so divine.
A cat stole my yarn, now it's tangled and bold,
My sweater's a monster, but hey, it's pure gold.

Socks chase each other, in a mad laundry chase,
Who knew that the dryer had its own little space?
A patch here, a patch there, it's quite the wild feast,
As I wear my mishmash, I'm the fashion's beast!

Between Gaps and Shadows

In the corner of rooms, where dust bunnies play,
I search for the meaning, but it's hiding away.
Empty mugs and old socks, they giggle and cheer,
They know all the secrets that they hold so dear.

The clock laughs at time, as it ticks with a grin,
It's a race with the cat, who'll lose, where to begin?
With shadows as friends, we dance in the night,
Finding joy in the gaps, what a comical sight!

The Colors of Uncertainty

A canvas of colors, they splash and they squirt,
I drop a can of paint, oh man! What a spurt!
Orange mixes with green, it's a sight most absurd,
Art is subjective, I've simply concurred.

Choices like crayons, they scatter and roll,
Do I go for the sun, or the glittery coal?
In this swirl of hues, confusion's a game,
Yet every sip of coffee tastes oddly the same.

Harmony in Chaos

In the chaos of dishes piled high in the sink,
I ponder my world, ever changing, I think.
A spoon fights a fork, in a raucous debate,
While I contemplate order, it can wait, it's just fate.

Zooming through life like a squirrel in hot pursuit,
Trying to find balance, I'm stuck in the loot.
With laughter the soundtrack, a whimsical show,
In this theater of madness, we dance to and fro!

The Search for Wholeness

In the drawer, I found a sock,
A wiry mess, a ticking clock.
Where's my other shoe, I plead,
Lost in the chaos, it's my creed.

I examine the couch, what a sight,
Change and crumbs, all piled tight.
A jigsaw of lost items here,
Who needs pieces? I need a beer!

The fridge beeps with a funny tune,
A lonely egg, it's over the moon.
The milk's expired, oh what a shame,
A puzzle so odd, it's a silly game.

Life's a dance with missing parts,
We laugh it off as silly arts.
Each hunt we take turns comical,
Finding the fit is such a spectacle!

Threads of Time

In my closet, time has stopped,
Sweaters big and pants adopted.
This shirt once fit, but now it lies,
Like a mystery, with shocked surprise.

At the mall, I try on clothes,
But my reflection inwardly groans.
A fit suggests some lost romance,
Threads unravel in a wild dance.

The calendar's a dusty book,
With dates forgotten, take a look.
I search for moments, where they hide,
Just hanging out like a bad guide.

Yet in this mess, a chuckle finds,
Joy exists in tangled twines.
With laughter shared, we're dressed divine,
Even if our style's out of line!

Pieces of a Dream

Last night I dreamed I flew so high,
But woke to find I can't even try.
My blanket's tangled, I can't escape,
A circus clown, without the cape.

Those ambitious plans on paper bright,
Turn to dust in morning light.
Where's the plot? And why the fuss?
I tripped on dreams — who knew it'd crush?

I mix up puzzles, switch the spots,
Chasing chimeras, who's counting dots?
Each fragment brings me silly schemes,
Yet still I float on waffled dreams.

With a laugh, I stitch each seam,
Waking up to a whimsical theme.
Life's a draft, let's monetize,
As laughter lifts us through the skies!

The Unfitted Bit

Under the couch, a rogue toast lies,
Its crusty coat, no wonder why.
I search for butter, there's none in sight,
I guess I'll eat it, what a plight!

The kitchen's a maze, what a chore!
Last week's dinner is now folklore.
With spills and thrills, I try to mend,
My culinary skills — a comical trend.

Each mismatched sock, a story bold,
In the laundry room, a treasure told.
I grin at chaos, mixed and matched,
In the unfitted bits, joy is hatched.

We puzzle through this daily grind,
Finding laughter in what we find.
With every slip, and every joke,
We build our world, so let's evoke!

Searching for Solace

In a box stacked high of mismatched dreams,
The cat plays fetch with my missing seams.
I swear it was here, just a moment ago,
Now it's lost in the couch, with my sanity too!

With a laugh and a sigh, I dig through the mess,
Unraveling socks, which add to my stress.
I'll find that piece, it must be around,
Maybe it's hiding where lost socks are found!

Orchestrating the Fragments

I'm a conductor of bits, with a baton made of cheese,
Each corner I seek brings me down to my knees.
I chase shadows and laughs, through a whimsical resort,
Where puzzle pieces laugh, at my frantic retort.

A parrot squawks, 'Try the fridge for your luck!'
I open it wide and find only a duck.
'Quack me a corner!' I shout through the din,
As the pieces all giggle, let the chaos begin!

Navigating the Labyrinth

I stroll through the maze, guided by whims,
Where missing edges make it hard to win.
A sign points 'This way!' but leads to a wall,
As squirrels debate if I'd like to join their ball.

I've traded my map for a slice of good pie,
And found that the journey's the reason I try.
With a dance and a jig, I embrace every turn,
For the path to the piece is the lesson I learn!

The Edge of Understanding

Balancing wits on the edge of my chair,
I ponder the mysteries that float in the air.
A wiggle, a wiggle, is it here, is it there?
Perhaps I should ask my pet hamster for care!

From boiling ideas to pies in the sky,
I gather my tools—a smile and a pie.
I'll fit in the pieces, as the giggles resound,
At the edge of confusion, my sanity's found!

Mapping the Unknown Paths

In the maze of morning snacks,
Lost my way with crumbs on tracks.
Got a sandwich, called it fate,
But mustard's tang just sealed my fate.

In the puzzle of mismatched socks,
I find the left with a pair of rocks.
One's striped, the other's polka-dot,
Fashion's choice? I think not!

Chasing down the cat with glee,
Thought she'd help me find the key.
But she just sat and licked her paw,
Guess the puzzle's got no law.

In a world of coffee spills,
I mix it up with chocolate thrills.
Life's a game of guess and play,
Just smile and roll with the display.

When Pieces Speak

Once a jigsaw spoke to me,
'This corner's where you want to be!'
But when I searched for edges neat,
I found a dog had made a treat.

Tangled in a yarn of tears,
Knitting breaks my love for cheers.
A scarf that grows and shrinks each time,
A perfect fit? I can't define!

At the store, I lost my way,
Thought I'd find the perfect play.
But all the games just fell apart,
Turns out I need a crafty heart!

With the calendar's dates a mess,
I've embraced my tangled stress.
Each time I plan, it falls awry,
But what's a laugh without a try?

Echoes of the Soul

I lost my sock, it danced away,
Under the couch, it went to play.
The cat was laughing, oh what a sight,
While I searched for it into the night.

My keys are hiding, playing peekaboo,
Under a pile of laundry, who knew?
They giggle softly, so out of reach,
Why can't they stay put, can't they teach?

Threads of Destiny

Spaghetti noodles all over the floor,
Like a treasure map, I must explore.
Sauce stains laughing, they won't go away,
I guess tonight is takeout day!

Cereal box is empty, what a drag,
But the prize toy's just a ragged rag.
I'll make a hat, or maybe a sail,
With plans like these, I cannot fail!

Shards of Serenity

My morning coffee spills with glee,
It whispers secrets, just to me.
The mug laughs as it falls, oh dear!
Guess today's theme is 'slippery' cheer.

Toothpaste on the mirror, what a scene,
A dental masterpiece, oh so keen!
I'm an artist now, with brushy streaks,
Who knew mornings could be so unique?

The Lost Piece

I looked for my remote, what a quest,
It's a shapeshifter, it won't let me rest.
Between the cushions, it plays hide and seek,
Lurking with snacks that I dare not peek.

The pet bird's mocking, flapping away,
As I tumble and tumble in disarray.
Maybe the puzzle piece's at the fair,
Riding the Ferris wheel, without a care!

Whispers in the Silence

In a room full of chatter, I found a sock,
It whispered secrets, but not quite a clock.
The cat looked puzzled, her tail in the air,
As I tried to decipher that enigmatic hair.

The fridge spoke loudly, with a flickering light,
Reminding me kindly of dinner last night.
I shushed the toaster, it popped out a grin,
Wondering why eggs were always so thin.

Missing Threads

In my sweater, a hole, oh what a delight,
It dances in breezes, a threadbare fright.
I search for a needle, alas, it's just me,
A seamstress of chaos, but nothing to see.

The carpet is rippling, with stories to tell,
Of crumbs from the past that now inhabit hell.
My trusty old couch seems to sigh in despair,
As it swallows my snacks like it's a big bear.

Facing the Fragmentation

I found a lost puzzle piece under my shoe,
It laughed at my forehead, it wasn't so blue.
The coffee mug giggled, its handle askew,
As I spilled all my thoughts with a splash and a zoo.

The TV's out dancing, it's on channel me,
And my remote's playing hide-and-seek with my tea.
A spoon joined the party, with forks in the air,
As I balanced them all without a single care.

The Spectrum of Solitude

I sat down to ponder, with a pencil and paw,
But the dog had ideas that broke every law.
He nudged me for treats while I scribbled a dream,
And the cat simply laughed at my silent regime.

A jigsaw of moments, bits scattered and free,
Danced in my thoughts like a kooky marquee.
In the end, I discovered with a chuckle so wide,
That solitude's party had an oops on the side.

Cryptic Connections

A sock goes missing, what a surprise,
The cat seems pleased, with glint in its eyes.
I search the drawers and under the bed,
Only to find it stuck, out of my head.

Puzzles of life, they twist and they turn,
Like my morning coffee, too hot to discern.
I add just a dash of sugar and cream,
Now it's all chaos, or so it would seem.

The toaster's on strike, what could it mean?
Bread is the answer, though seldom seen.
Meanwhile, I ponder on tales of the day,
Where all the lost things have hidden away.

Clocks tick in rhythm, with silly chimes,
Counting the moments and skipping the times.
As I sort my thoughts, like jumbled toys,
Laughter erupts with all of its joys.

Where Pieces Collide

Gather the bits, the odds and the ends,
What remains is chaos, no need to pretend.
My fridge has a mystery, a science project,
A questionable scent, I must interject.

I journey through shops, like a puzzler's quest,
Searching for answers, but missing the rest.
The cereal aisle, a reflective affair,
Where marshmallows dance in the cool morning air.

Yet here comes a phone call, a number I know,
Just spam, I laugh, it's all part of the flow.
Mom asks 'Are you well?' while I munch my toast,
I want to say yes, but I'm searching the most.

In the end it's simple, a laugh and a grin,
The pieces might fit, or they just might spin.
With every twist, I embrace the surprise,
As more silly riddles arise with the pies.

Beneath the Surface

Wrestling with dreams beneath afternoon suns,
Trying to find where the laughter begins.
A sock in the dryer, yes, it's quite odd,
You'd think it'd be simple, but I nod and just plod.

Under the couch lives the storied dust bunnies,
Each one a relic from moments quite funny.
They dance in the shadows, a sight to behold,
Whispering secrets that never get told.

The cat plots revenge, on a rubber band spree,
As I chase it around, laughing light-heartedly.
In a world turned topsy, where whimsy abounds,
We stumble and fumble, yet joy often sounds.

Underneath it all, there's a gleam and a blink,
Past the absurd, we find time to rethink.
With good friends beside me, we'll piece it all tight,
Making sense of nonsense, beneath the moonlight.

The Hidden Link

Cracked mugs and old socks are friends in disguise,
In the land of mismatches, where laughter complies.
A jigsaw of memories, tossed in a heap,
Where humor's the key, and the quirks never sleep.

I scoop up the crumbs of each witty exchange,
These moments, like candy, are remarkably strange.
They stick to your soul like the gum on the floor,
A delightful reminder of what's at the core.

The dog's got a ball, that's a shoe and a sock,
He races through puddles, then slops on the rock.
Each gallant splash brings a giggle or two,
As I watch all this chaos, I wonder anew.

Perhaps it's the chaos that brings us the cheer,
In the mix of our troubles, we find what is dear.
So here's to the links, hidden right in plain sight,
In the mishaps and giggles, everything feels right.

Map of Disparate Paths

In search of directions, I take a glance,

The GPS laughs, says, "Go on, take a chance!"
It points to the left, then says, "No, to the right,"
But somehow I'm stuck, in a roundabout night.

The road sings a tune, but I'm tone-deaf for sure,
Each fork in the road just adds to my blur.
With signs pointing sideways and detours galore,
I'm certain my map's been dropped on the floor.

The Hidden Fit

I search in the drawer for a sock that will pair,
But there's just a lone one, a fabric affair.
"Where's your friend gone?" I holler with glee,
But it hides in the wash with a cheer for its spree.

The puzzle is missing, or so it appears,
I find joy in chaos and laughter in tears.
Those mismatched old socks tell tales of their quest,
In the game of connection, they still are the best.

Discovering Wholeness in Pieces

A cup here, a fork there, I skip and I slide,
Trying to cook breakfast with tools I can't find.
While missing the bowl, I whip eggs with a grin,
I serve up a cake, and it's messy, but win!

With candor and chaos, I dance on the floor,
As flour flies wildly and spills out the door.
Though it's not quite a feast, it's a laughable thing,
In the world of odd morsels, joy is the king.

Assembly Required: Heart Edition

A flat-pack for feelings—what a strange thrill,
It comes with a manual, but gives me a chill.
With screws and odd bits, I attempt to create,
But the heart's a soft piece—oh, what a first date!

Instructions are vague; I try twisting and turning,
But the pieces resist, as my heart starts to learn.
In the end, I assemble a love that's a mix,
A jumble of laughter, with a few silly tricks.

The Confluence of Parts

In a box so bright and wide,
Are pieces that do not abide.
Some are round, others square,
Why can't they all just share?

The cat thinks it's a game,
While I wrestle with the same.
Last week, I had a fight,
With a piece that vanished from sight.

How's a triangle supposed to fit,
With a jam of squares, I admit?
Where's that edge, I can't recall,
Was it hiding behind the wall?

Amidst the chaos I make my stand,
Creating art, so unplanned.
Sure, it's crooked, but it's mine,
With mismatched parts, I dine divine!

Dance of the Disparate

A circle spun with flair and grace,
Jumps in and takes up space.
A line says, 'You're in my way!'
The round just laughs and sways!

One piece says it's too fat,
The other claims it's a hat.
They twirl and spin, what a sight,
Inventing shapes through sheer delight!

Oh, the square looks quite confused,
Why's no one wearing shoes?
The dance floor's quite the scene,
Made of pieces never seen!

When the music starts to fade,
They line up—oh how they've played!
Not a corner in the bunch,
Yet they fit in, what a punch!

Navigating the Empty Spots

I set my sail on a sea of gaps,
With floating bits and silly laps.
Where's the piece that holds it tight?
I search by day, I dream by night.

A noodle wiggles, a triangle squeaks,
Between the gaps, a buddy peaks.
"Hey, want to join this merry crew?"
I shrug and say, "Sure, why not you?"

The corners giggle at my plight,
As I search for anchor in their flight.
"Don't take it too hard," a starfish said,
"You're better off with dreams instead!"

So I float with pieces bright,
Making boats of sheer delight.
Embracing spaces, I take a shot,
At a masterpiece—whatever I've got!

The Illusion of Wholeness

Here's a galaxy that doesn't align,
Where bits and bobs think they can shine.
They claim to fit and promise tight,
But I know that they're not quite right.

A piece shouts, "I'm the captain here!"
While another rolls and disappears.
They argue over who's the star,
While I contemplate just how bizarre!

With each attempt, they say, "Relax,"
While I draft up an escape plan fax.
The puzzle's rules seem quite absurd,
But oh, how loud the laughter stirred!

So I sit with pieces mismatched,
In laughter's glow, we're all attached.
The goal isn't whole; it's quite a game,
In this delightful, jumbled frame!

Mosaic of Moments

In a jumble of socks, I search with glee,
Matching the patterns, oh where can they be?
One's striped and the other, a bright polka dot,
Together they laugh, in a wardrobe spot.

Coffee on Monday, spills on my shirt,
It's the style I picked, to avoid the dirt.
My hair's in a twist, oh what a grand mess,
Yet through all the chaos, I still feel blessed.

Every mishap, a part of the plan,
Each laugh and each cry, makes me who I am.
Silly little moments, like bubbles that pop,
Crafting a picture, I won't let it stop.

From crumbs on the floor to a search for the keys,
I dance through the day with humor and ease.
So here's to the bits that don't make any sense,
They fit in the puzzle; it's all happened hence!

Finding Harmony in Chaos

The cat on the table, the dog in my lap,
They're orchestrating chaos; what a funny trap!
A symphony played with the clang of a spoon,
In this wild concert, I'm over the moon.

Dishes are singing, the laundry's in tune,
While the vacuum hums a soft afternoon.
Stumbling on toys like a joyful parade,
Life's energetic ballet, I've lovingly made.

Juggling my snacks as I slip on a shoe,
Tripping on rhythms, a dance that's brand new.
Every mishap a note in my vibrant song,
Melodies tangled where all of us belong.

So let's toss the rules, let chaos reign bright,
In a world where we twirl like a kite in the light.
With laughter our compass, we'll strut and we'll spin,
Finding harmony in the madness we're in!

Unraveling the Enigma

A sock and a shoe, where could they roam?
In the maze of the laundry, they've built a new home.
One's under the bed, the other won't talk,
They'll keep their secrets, just like a catwalk.

I search for my keys in a pile of old mail,
Deciphering patterns like some ancient tale.
Scissors lost in the couch, a remote in the fridge,
Finding each item feels like a grand bridge.

Pancakes that flip with a little too much flair,
End up on ceilings — oh, what a rare air!
The syrup drips slowly, like time on a shelf,
In this riddle of moments, I laugh at myself.

Each clue that I gather is frosting on cake,
A spritz of a riddle, some laughter to make.
Though the answers are jumbled, scattered like breeze,
I smile at the chaos; it's all just a tease!

Shape of Existence

A sandwich gone rogue, its toppings all spill,
Tomato and lettuce, they dance on the grill.
I chase after bites like a butterfly's flit,
In this gourmet game, I'm not ready to quit.

The clock takes a break, as I nap on the floor,
My dreams are full of snacks, and maybe some more.
Life's shapeshifting form is a wibble and wobble,
I grin at the quirky; I'd never just squabble.

Puzzles of veggies on my plate in a swirl,
Broccoli trees and carrots that twirl.
With each joyful bite, I unravel the fun,
In this quirky banquet, I never would run!

So here's to the zany shapes life has in store,
Each moment a piece I'll happily adore.
With laughter our glue, in this colorful scene,
We shape our existence; it's all quite a dream!

Navigating Life's Labyrinth

I lost my way in a maze of cheese,
Turns out, I'm allergic to Swiss with ease.
I tried to find a door made of bread,
But all I found was a cat on the bed.

Where's the guide, or the map, or the clue?
My compass just spins, is it broken too?
I ask the bird, it just shrugs with glee,
"Maybe the secret is just being free!"

With twists and turns, it's a silly race,
A funhouse mirror with a smiling face.
I tripped on a shoe left by someone tall,
It's a wild adventure, after all!

So here I wander, in this zany land,
With a rubber chicken and an ice cream stand.
Each step reveals a sight so bizarre,
Life's quirks and giggles, our shining star!

The Shape of What's to Come

Life's a shape that's oddly drawn,
I asked a crayon at the break of dawn.
It said, "Draw circles, squares, and lines,
Just avoid the spots where the sunlight shines!"

I tried my best to sketch with flair,
But ended up tangled in my own hair.
The triangle laughed; the circle rolled,
While the square just sat, looking bold.

With every twist, I scribble and spin,
A wobbly ride where we've all been.
"Embrace the mess and let it flow,"
Said the squiggly worm with a twinkling glow.

So I'll color outside the lines today,
Embracing chaos in a vibrant way.
Each shape will dance, and each color won't miss,
Creating a future, wondrous and bliss!

When Pieces Align

In a jigsaw world, I lost a part,
It rolled away with a puff and a start.
I searched the fridge and under the bed,
Found only moldy bread instead.

The cat intervened with a flick of the tail,
"Finding that piece is quite the tale!"
So we grabbed some snacks and made a plan,
To conquer this mess, as best as we can.

With laughter and snacks, it became clear,
The missing piece was the fun we share here.
So here's to the moments, however they land,
In the dance of the puzzle, we'll take a stand!

Every twist and turn brings such delight,
When pieces align, it's sheer dynamite.
So let's keep searching, and when we do fine,
Let's party with joy—it's puzzle-solving time!

Discovering the Hidden Connections

I looked for links like a great detective,
Found socks in the fridge and toys quite selective.
The dog gave a wink, and the cat gave a purr,
In this odd household, it's a bit of a blur.

I texted my neighbor, "Hey, where's the glue?"
He replied, "It's stuck to my shoe, it's true!"
With every mix-up, we giggle and laugh,
Creating strange bonds like a quirky giraffe.

Life's silly tangles are knots that we weave,
Like a juggler's show, who'd never believe,
That hidden connections, both odd and profound,
Are the treasures and laughter that we have found.

So here's to the quirks and the strange turns we take,
In this crazy adventure, let's dance and partake.
With each silly mishap and every new twist,
We'll celebrate connections that no one could miss!

The Quest for Completion

I searched high and low, what a sight,
For a piece that fits just right.
Under the couch, behind the chair,
A puzzle piece? No, just my dog's hair.

With friends we gather, chips in hand,
"I've got the piece!" I proudly stand.
But as I celebrate, my buddy sighs,
Turns out it's just a snack size fry!

The corner seems lost, nowhere to find,
My puzzle's a mess, but who's in a bind?
Laughter erupts as we give it a go,
We're in stitches, not caring for flow.

So here's to the search, the joy we create,
In the hunt for the piece, we celebrate fate.
Forget about edges, let's make this a blast,
With giggles and grins, it's fun unsurpassed.

Reflections in Pieces

I looked in the mirror, what did I see?
A jigsaw of laughter staring back at me.
One eye's a puzzle, the nose is too wide,
Even my hair, what a jumbled ride!

My friend tried to help with a little advice,
"Just flip it around, it'll be nice!"
But every rotation just gives me a fright,
Am I a portrait or abstract tonight?

We giggle as colors confuse every line,
This hilarious chaos, oh it's truly divine!
Embracing the edges, we carry the cheer,
Making our own art, because why not, dear?

So here's to reflections that twist and that turn,
Life's a fun riddle, let's savor and learn.
With friendship, the laughter will always align,
In a world of confusion, we're doing just fine.

The Missing Ingredient

I'm baking a cake, oh what a delight,
But wait, where's the egg? It's out of sight!
Flour and sugar, they're all in a trance,
Without my dear egg, I can't take a chance.

I rummaged the fridge with a curious glee,
Found mustard and pickles, but where's my key?
My cake's now a salad, a wild mix indeed,
I guess I'll just laugh, 'cause it's all that I need.

So, here's to the bakers who dream big and bold,
With things that they find, never left in the cold.
Each missing ingredient becomes a new dish,
With a dash of humor, it's all that I wish.

In kitchens of chaos, we simmer and stir,
What's missing? Just giggles, all we require.
From batter to bliss, we've tossed in a twist,
As long as we're laughing, it's pure gourmet bliss.

Journey Beyond the Edges

Pack up your bags, we're off on a trip,
Chasing those corners, let's take a big sip.
With friends by my side and snacks all around,
We'll venture beyond, where fun can be found.

The road is a puzzle, twisty and bendy,
Every stop we make feels oddly trendy.
We dance at the rest stops, sing loud with glee,
Not lost but exploring—oh, can't you see?

Around every corner, new laughter unfolds,
Our memories shaping like stories retold.
With maps made of giggles, we lose track of time,
This journey we're on? It's truly sublime!

So here's to the wanderers, finders of fun,
In the search for the edges, adventures begun.
With spirits so high, and smiles so wide,
We'll cherish these moments as joy will abide.

Kaleidoscope of Being

Colors swirl, a dizzying dance,
Lost in patterns, not a second glance.
Chasing shadows around the bend,
Who knew confusion could be a friend?

Jigsaw pieces from different sets,
Lamenting our humorous regrets.
Trying to fit where we don't belong,
Laughing at notes to an off-key song.

Crayons melt in the summer's heat,
Melodies played by a stumbling feat.
In the chaos, a giggle takes flight,
Mismatched socks are a fashion delight!

Twisting and turning, we take a chance,
A joyful misstep, life's crazy dance.
Finding fun in the wild and weird,
It's all just a laugh—so don't be steered!

Aligning the Misaligned

Corkscrew thoughts all tangled and tight,
Spaghetti noodles on a plate at night.
Looking for order, it's all a blur,
Maybe a cat will give us the cure?

Wobbly chairs and misplaced dreams,
Life's not as simple as it first seems.
Juggling socks while baking a pie,
Who put the oven up there — oh my!

Cracks in the sidewalk lead to new paths,
Counting the echoes of our loud laughs.
Misaligned fenders on a rusty bike,
Riding through chaos like *Riders of the Strikes*!

Fuzzy directions on a treasure map,
Searching for gold in a friendly gap.
Aligning the misaligned with flair,
Let's laugh at the thorns, but still stop and stare!

Portraits of Disarray

Splattered paint on a canvas wide,
A rabbit in socks trying to hide.
Portraits of madness, a tangle of cheer,
Delighted embraces of random fear.

Socks on the ceiling, fish in a tree,
Questions abound: why are they free?
Chaotic brush strokes, a masterpiece sprawled,
In the arms of absurdity, we stand enthralled.

Twists in the story, plots gone askew,
Behold the mayhem in every hue.
Laughter erupts, a delightful parade,
Just hold on tight—don't be afraid!

Capturing madness in snapshots bright,
Finding the joy in the silly and slight.
Each disarray, a moment to share,
In the gallery of life, we all play fair!

The Quest for Clarity

Whimsical maps lead us astray,
Chasing the setting sun every day.
Markers are faded, directions unclear,
Arriving for tea—wait, not for beer!

Foggy perceptions like marshmallow fluff,
Looking for answers but told, 'Not enough!'
Finding the jest in our serious quests,
A squirrel in a suit is the best of jest!

Fuzzy binoculars block out the view,
Squinting at signs that say, 'Not for you.'
With each wrong turn, the laughter unfolds,
Tracking the breadcrumbs like treasure from old.

The quest for clarity, a glitch in the plan,
But oh, what a sight—an acrobatic man!
In every mishap, there's gold to be found,
Navigating chaos, the fun knows no bound!

Conundrum of the Everyday

In the morning, socks don't match,
Coffee spills with every catch.
The toast pops up, a joyful sound,
Where's my car? Oh, lost and found!

The keys are hiding, little rascals,
Under pillows, in the bristles.
The cat has claimed the laundry mound,
And I'm still searching all around!

A sandwich falls, the dog creeps near,
With a grin that shows no fear.
An empty jar, it shouts, 'Just eat!'
Then laughs at me with every repeat.

Yet in chaos, laughter's found,
In little slips and tumbling round.
Oh, what fun this day can bring,
In all the mess, I hear joy sing!

The Frame of Our Story

We've hung our hats on crooked hooks,
And filed our plans by storybooks.
An adventure waits—where should we go?
But first, let's find where the snacks stow!

With crayons lost beneath the bed,
And puzzles mixed with thoughts unsaid.
Our frame is cracked but oh so bright,
Each memory shared, a pure delight.

Cheese sticks serve as makeshift swords,
While laughter reigns in full accords.
The corners blur, at times we stray,
Yet every twist's a brand new way!

So let's rejoice in what we seek,
The silly tales, the moments meek.
Together, we find joy unplanned,
In our quirky, jumbled land!

Fragmented Whispers

In whispers soft, the tales unfold,
Of socks that vanish, treasures bold.
The printer's jammed with paper woe,
Yet laughter dances, high and low.

My phone rings bright, it's on my head!
Where's my breakfast? Oh, I'm misled.
The cat meows like she's a queen,
As bowls are filled—oh what a scene!

A puzzle piece, one tiny shard,
Found in the fridge, it's quite bizarre!
The dog has chewed the remnant fine,
It's part of art, or so I pine!

Amid the quirks, I find delight,
In croaking frogs and candlelight.
For in this chaos, laughs arise,
As fragments whisper, curious sighs!

The Missing Edge

The search begins for missing bits,
In drawers piled with all the splits.
A half-eaten snack, a puzzle gone,
Squirrels hoarding; oh, moving on!

One shoe in blue, the other red,
Who dressed me this? A mystery, bred.
The clock strikes two, but where's my phone?
It's making calls—now I feel alone!

The cat thinks it's her jungle gym,
As I crawl searching up to the brim.
Yet in the hunt, I start to see,
That laughter fits quite perfectly!

So here's to missing bits and pieces,
Our days are fun, and joy never ceases.
With every edge that goes awry,
We piece together life's sweet pie!

Edges and Angles of the Soul

In a box marked 'fun', I sift and I sort,
Hoping for pieces that match, not distort.
A triangle giggles, a circle just spins,
While the square looks so grumpy like it just can't win.

I turn over bits with a curious grin,
Is this one a side? Or maybe a fin?
I'm laughing at corners that won't fit, oh dear!
My jigsaw's a party, let's all grab a beer!

It's chaos, it's color, a wild little dance,
As I chase after edges that won't take a chance.
My cat thinks it's magic, she pounces and plays,
As I piece together this mix-up of days.

But oh, what a joy when a corner aligns,
A sliver of sanity hidden in lines.
So here's to the angles that make us feel whole,
And the silly confusion, the quirks of the soul.

Completing the Unseen Picture

I've got pieces of clouds, and a slice of a sun,
A patchwork of giggles, oh, this could be fun!
A chip of a memory, a dab of pure glee,
I'm on the lookout for what's missing in me.

In the drawer of dreams, my puzzle resides,
With mismatched intentions, and twisty guides.
A fork and a spoon, now that's quite appealing,
As I grab for the pieces, I'm laughing, revealing.

Each part tells a story, some wacky and wild,
Like a doodle of childhood, a whimsical child.
I can't find the edge of this colorful mess,
But it's so much more fun than I could ever guess.

So I gather the bits, without a clear plan,
In this gallery of chaos, I'm a yes man.
Let's celebrate fragments, as they dance in delight,
Completing the unseen, we'll get it just right!

Searching for the Missing Edge

On a quest for that edge, I'm putting in time,
With bags full of whimsy and the odd bit of rhyme.
Why's the sky blue? Why so many squares?
As I hunt for my corner, I'm brushing my hairs.

The fridge has some magnets, a fork in the draw,
The toaster has stories that leave me in awe.
Where did my right piece wander off to tonight?
Maybe it's hiding in plain view, bold and bright.

I chat with my socks and the cat gives me sass,
'You think it's a puzzle? Just look at the grass!'
There's magic in chaos, and joy in the chase,
For every lost piece, there's a grin on my face.

So here's to the hunt, let's embrace all the fun,
With laughter and quirks, I'm never outdone.
Each missing edge is a laugh still in store,
In this game of confusion, I'm loving it more!

Collage of Tomorrow's Hopes

I gather my dreams in a big jumbo heap,
With stickers of rainbows that dance and that leap.
A fragment of laughter, a sprinkle of cheer,
In a collage of hopes, ain't nothing to fear.

The scissors called 'Future' are clumsy and bold,
While the glue named 'Today' sticks stories untold.
I paste on a smile, a slice of each wish,
In a puzzle of moments, I whip up a dish.

Each piece tells of laughter, some slip and some slide,
As I gather my gems from the wild, silly ride.
The corners may be missing, but oh what a view!
When the heart is all stitched, there's magic anew.

So let's throw confetti and dance through the night,
For every lost corner shines vibrant and bright.
In this collage of tomorrows, I find my way clear,
With hopes all around me, there's nothing to fear!

Building Bridges

In a world of arches and beams,
Frogs may quite jump in teams.
Sometimes we trip on our own shoelace,
But laughter keeps us in the race.

On the road of connecting dots,
You'll find wobbly chairs and pots.
With duct tape and a little cheer,
We can fix our wayward sphere.

Silly paths may lead the way,
To wobbly joys we'll sway and play.
A bridge made of candy and cheer,
Brings everyone together here.

So grab your tools, just a few,
And build a bridge—yes, you can too!
Through silly slips and joyful clinks,
Together, we'll find what life thinks.

Cracked but Not Broken

A coffee cup with a little chip,
Still holds warmth, let's take a sip.
With every crack, there's room for glee,
Like a funky dance or a buzzing bee.

Life drips a little from the seam,
Yet we bounce, as if in a dream.
Wobble, wobble, who needs straight?
Cracked porcelain can still look great!

Laughter echoes through the cracks,
Witty jabs and playful hacks.
Each little flaw's a badge of pride,
In our mad, wondrous ride.

So raise a toast to the silly sides,
With cracked cups, let's go for rides.
We may wobble, we may sway,
But we're alive, come what may!

Realm of the Incomplete

In a kingdom of bits and bobs,
Some pages lost from our own jobs.
A jigsaw with missing pieces seems,
Like life's a comic of half-formed dreams.

Fridges hum with weird delights,
While socks play hide and seek at nights.
An incomplete puzzle pops and fizzles,
As we gather laughter's whizzles.

With mismatched socks, an artful stroll,
We embrace it all, that's our goal.
A treasure hunt on a jigsaw mat,
Finding joy in the wild and scat!

Incomplete, yet so divine,
We laugh and dance, sip some wine.
In this quirky, silly show,
Each little gap lets our joy grow!

The Heart of the Matter

In the chest of a chicken rests the soul,
Why did it cross? To reach a goal!
Underneath a circus tent we thrive,
With juggling hearts, the show's alive!

The meat of our tales can be quite juicy,
Even when life feels a little loosey-goosey.
With laughter as our guiding star,
We'll frolic and skip, no matter how far.

Worms in the heart? Don't squirm, don't fret,
Just dance a little, don't place a bet.
In the matter of hearts, there's always fire,
Let humor light up our wild desire.

So strike a pose, do a funny dance,
Let whimsy play, take a chance!
The heart of the matter is shiny and bright,
In this world of chaos, we find our light.

Cartography of Human Hearts

In the map of love, we're all lost,
Each heart a compass, counting the cost.
We zigzag through laughter, causing a stir,
As GPS fails, we fumble and blur.

Navigating emotions, we trip on our feet,
Google can't find where we seek out the sweet.
Sketchy directions, we laugh 'til we cry,
The road is a riddle, yet off we fly.

With markers of joy and bumps from the tears,
Our routes are a mix of giggles and fears.
In maps of affection, the corners are round,
Yet somehow together, we still feel profound.

Wander we must, in this wild game of chance,
GPS or not, we all love to dance.
Though lost in translation, the journey's a blast,
With every wrong turn, we're free—what a cast!

The Cornerstone of Our Journeys

On roads paved with snacks and odd little charms,
We build our foundations, snug in each other's arms.
Every misstep we take, it makes for a tale,
As we stumble through life, giggling without fail.

The corners we search, often hiding in plain sight,
Are filled with ice cream and questionable bites.
With layers of laughter, we stack up our dreams,
Where quirky ideas burst at the seams.

In this merry parade of mismatched shoes,
We strut through the puddles, not caring to lose.
Each step's an encore, a play in disguise,
As we trip over smiles that light up the skies.

Navigating chaos, we dance 'round our fears,
With colorful crayons that wipe out the tears.
Though our paths may diverge, love's the sweet glue,
In our playful pursuits, it connects me to you!

Fitting In and Breaking Free

In a box made of laughter, we're shapes that are odd,
Twisting and turning, we stumble like frogs.
Some fit like a glove, others don't quite belong,
But we all find a place—come on, join the song!

Like puzzle pieces painted in vibrant array,
We battle conformity, hip-hip-hooray!
With every misfit twist, we giggle and cheer,
Breaking down walls while sharing a beer.

The corners can wiggle, and edges may fray,
As we dance in the chaos of each funny day.
Embracing the quirks, we find our own style,
In the circus of life, let's float for a while.

So here's to the moments we laugh and we shake,
The crazy connections that only we make.
In a world so precise, we'll shine like a star,
In the art of the odd—the best kind of bizarre!

Each Piece Holds a Secret

Every oddchunk forgotten, tucked under the bed,
Holds whispers of stories that float in our head.
Like socks that get lost in the wash of the night,
Each piece that we gather, a dance in delight.

Clipping and clapping, we search through the clues,
For hidden adventures, our life's tangled views.
We piece them together, though some don't align,
They fill in the gaps with sweet humor divine.

In treasure hunts crazy, with dogs that run wild,
We find silly treasures, just like a child.
Every goof in our lives adds color and spice,
A patchwork of giggles, oh, isn't it nice?

So gather your secrets and spin them with flair,
In the quilt of the curious, we all have a share.
For every odd piece that makes you complete,
In the game of existence, we conquer, we meet!

Jigsaw of Dawn and Dusk

Morning's bright with scattered cheer,
Yet pieces hide, they disappear.
Where's the slice of toast for me?
Oh look, a cat! But where's the key?

Evening falls, the sun takes flight,
Missing bits lost in the night.
A squiggly piece that seems to fit,
Or was it just an old dog's bit?

Day and night, they play their game,
Seeking parts more wild than tame.
A cheeky grin, a wink, a bow,
Who knew this chaos was just how?

In shadows long and giggles bright,
Frame the mishaps with pure delight.
So grab a snack, we're on a quest,
This funny piecework is the best!

The Art of Assembling Dreams

Scattered thoughts, like socks on floors,
Adventures wait behind closed doors.
One piece glimmers, with a wink,
Is it a dream? Or just a stink?

A canvas full of jumbled hues,
With painted skies and broccoli blues.
Where's that orange? Ah! Here it lies,
Oh, wait, that's just a box of fries!

Crafting visions with silly schemes,
Where's the piece that fits our dreams?
A giggle here, a fumble there,
The masterpiece needs more hot air!

Just like life, it comes undone,
But let's laugh hard, it's all good fun.
So find that match, dance 'round the room,
In quirky art, let joy bloom!

Echoes in a Tattered Frame

In a frame that squeaks and groans,
Pieces chatter with silly tones.
What's that sound? A wiggle, a jig!
Maybe that's just my cat—he's big!

Old memories float, a parade of quirks,
Like mismatched socks that love to lurk.
A golden face with a silver base,
But crayons melted—a funny case!

Time's ticking loud, like a clock that's lost,
Searching for pieces, no matter the cost.
Yet laughter echoes, fills the air,
Who knew assembling dreams could be rare?

So flip the squares, give 'em a spin,
No rules apply when chaos begins.
Embrace the mess, frame it with glee,
In the tattered bits, we find a key!

Whispers of the Unfinished Scene

A canvas shy with hesitant strokes,
Shadows linger, the laughter pokes.
Where's the brush to make it whole?
Perhaps it's hiding in the doll's bowl!

Splashes here of green and red,
A tiger's face, but where's its head?
Puzzles spill like sugar's spread,
With bits of stories that we've read.

Look at this mess, a toddler's game,
Still, we giggle, it's all the same.
Fingers dance on edges and seams,
We build it up with our goofy dreams!

So join the fun, let laughter's grace,
Embrace the odd, we'll find our place.
An unfinished work, a silly tune,
Like singing with a raccoon under the moon!

Unseen Connections

In a box of scattered dreams,
The left shoe met a pair of beans.
A sock said, 'Why not join the show?'
A dance with a cat? Oh, what a glow!

An owl and a squirrel shared a drink,
Arguing if hats help one think.
The clock chimed twice, then took a trip,
While coffee mugs formed a friendship grip.

Palm trees wore shades, feeling so cool,
While a fish tried to learn how to drool.
Under the stars, they shared a laugh,
The moon winked, doing its math!

In a world of quirky sight,
Even pigeons wait for the bus at night.
Each piece a chuckle, a twist on fate,
Finding laughter in every state!

The Puzzle Within

A crab scuttled over a sandwich spread,
While ants had a rave, just dancing instead.
The napkin sighed, 'What a wild scene!'
As jelly danced, trying to be seen!

My keys were lost, but oh, not far,
Hiding beneath a singing guitar.
The cat suggested a game of charades,
While the fridge hummed its own escapades.

With puzzles in boxes and boxes in time,
A rubber band stretched, a flow so prime.
The rug erupted in giggles galore,
As slippers slipped out to explore!

So embrace the odd, the err, the goof,
Sometimes the missing piece is a roof.
With laughs and grins, we'll search anew,
For laughter's the force that sees us through!

Fragments of Truth

A toaster confided in a nearby plate,
'I'm burnt out, can't handle my fate!'
The butter chimed in, 'Let's stick together,'
While the jam spilled tales of sunny weather!

Puzzles were scattered like leaves in the breeze,
Jigsawing life with the greatest of ease.
A pirate parrot taught fish how to sail,
While a snail wrote each part of the tale.

Under the couch lived a sock puppet crew,
Dancing each night all cozied in blue.
With laughter they pieced together their night,
Finding joy in the odd and out of sight!

So let's puzzle together, you and I,
With a wink and a jig, we'll reach for the sky.
Every moment a fragment that shines so bright,
Life's a giggle; it's sheer delight!

Dancing Through Disarray

Amidst the clutter, the chaos swirled,
A disco ball spun, a new world unfurled.
Dust bunnies pranced with gusto and cheer,
While spoons did the cha-cha, oh so near!

Colorful socks held a fashion parade,
Debating their styles until night began to fade.
An umbrella twirled like it was on a spree,
As a book whispered, 'Let's make history!'

With giggles and wiggles, the world took flight,
As bananas formed a band under starlight.
Peanut butter drew a smile from toast,
And even a rock claimed to be the most!

So let's dance through the messy and wild,
With laughter and joy, forever compiled.
In the puzzling moments, we find our way,
Creating a tune where we all want to play!

Aligning the Stars

In the cosmos, stars misalign,
Chasing pieces, sipping on brine.
Constellations laugh, fall from grace,
Find the sigma in that vast space.

A dog chews on a missing plan,
While jellybeans dance, oh what a clamor!
The moon's a slice, the sun's a wink,
Twirling around like they don't think.

Coffee spills on a chart of fate,
Tickle the universe, don't wait!
A puzzle piece shaped like a pine,
Who needs order? Let's sip wine!

Yet in chaos, we find some fun,
Searching for meaning, 'neath the sun.
Glimmers of laughter, bits of bliss,
With each mix-up, we learn to twist.

The Art of Assembly

Building dreams with broken bits,
Laughter echoes, goofball skits.
A manual written by a cat,
But who needs guides? We're having a chat!

Lego towers of mismatched stacks,
A jigsaw form that just relax.
Wiggling pieces, oh what a dance,
Let's glue it all and take a chance!

The fork finds the knife, what's their deal?
A spatula claims it feels surreal.
They argue, yet the pudding's whipped,
In this kitchen, chaos is equipped.

Yet when the curtain rises high,
The pièce de résistance, oh my!
In disarray, we find our way—
The art of assembly brightens the day.

Restoring the Picture

Watch the canvas like a jester's grin,
Colors dance, where to begin?
With tape and dreams and a splash of glue,
Restoring a scene much askew!

The squirrel's stash is full of quirks,
Each acorn hides tons of perks.
A puzzle piece finds a hat to wear,
Behold the picture without a care!

A paintbrush whispers sweet nothings there,
While the canvas chuckles, beyond compare.
With each stroke, the past seems clear—
An artwork blooms, so rest your fear.

The colors clash, but oh what joy,
To piece together this wild toy!
In chaos found, we've made a kin—
Restoring pictures can make you grin!

Glimmers of Wholeness

Stray thoughts glitter like confetti dreams,
Wobbling around like mischievous beams.
One sock here, a shoe over there,
Glimmers of wholeness float in the air.

A puzzle box without a guide,
Tangled stories merge and slide.
A wobbly table of misfit chairs,
Cracking jokes like they're millionaires.

A rubber duck floats in the mix,
Making quacks, inventing new tricks.
With every slip, we find some grace,
Embracing life's wild, strange chase.

So raise a toast to that sunny spark,
In the heart of chaos, still leaves a mark.
Glimmers of wholeness shine so bright—
In the fun of being, all feels right!

Echoes of the Untold

In a world of scattered bits,
I chase my socks, where did they split?
Every drawer, a curious tale,
Whispers of where my other shoe's pale.

Coffee spills and crumbs galore,
I search for the snacks I swore!
Life's like a game of hide and seek,
Finding answers feels quite weak.

Laughter erupts in mismatched shoes,
Dancing puzzlers can't lose!
What fits where? A daily jest,
Makes it fun, forget the rest!

So let's embrace this quirky dance,
With mismatched pieces, take a chance!
The secret's in the fun we sew,
In tangled threads, imagination will grow.

Through the Cracks

Through the cracks in my old chair,
I find strange treasures, but beware!
Lost remote, a half-eaten snack,
Evidence of a life gone slack.

The cat thinks it's a game of fate,
Pouncing on mysteries, feeling great!
Mismatched puzzle, where's the start?
Guess it's just a work of art!

Laundry's a quest, where's that shirt?
Each sock's a soldier, filled with dirt.
Can't find the hole in my own plan,
But I'll make do, 'cause I can!

Laughter echoes in this clown parade,
Finding joy is never delayed!
So here's to the mess, let it be known,
Life's a carnival where humor's grown!

Weaving Reality

Threads of chaos, weaving fine,
A tapestry of lost designs.
Spilled pizza on my favorite shirt,
Pattern of stains, ain't that a perk?

Jigsaw dreams on a rainy day,
Where every piece seems far away.
Puzzle pieces double-cross,
But isn't that where we find the gloss?

Glue my plans with silly tape,
Glimmers of hope in every shape.
Puns and giggles fill the air,
Realities fray, but who's to care?

So let's spin this yarn of jest,
In colors bright, we're truly blessed!
Crafting tales in joyful seams,
Finding laughter in wild dreams!

The Final Touch

My masterpiece, a sight to behold,
But wait! I'm missing pieces of gold.
A spoon, a fork, oh what a twist,
Making gourmet out of a hit or miss!

The fridge is a chamber of surprise,
Necessities lurk in crafty disguise.
A half-drunk soda, a bit of cheese,
I'll whip up magic with great ease!

Last minute chaos, never dread,
For every mess, there's laughter fed.
The final touch, with a wink,
Stirring up joy, don't you think?

So here's to the odd and the strange,
Embracing quirks, no need to change!
In our mosaic, let's find delight,
A world of whimsy, shining bright!

Whirlwind of Assemblies

In a box filled with bright squares,
I sift through colors, with wild stares.
A piece that fits? A precious catch,
But all I find is a broken patch.

A cat jumps in, rubber duck swims,
I search for form in whimsical whims.
"Does this go there?" I slyly shout,
The puzzle laughs, I twist about.

I hold a triangle, it teases me,
Staring back as if it's free.
"Join me here, or dance in dreams?"
I grumble loud, "Nothing's as it seems!"

As time runs out, I take a sip,
Of lemonade—oops! A tiny slip.
The pieces scatter, laugh and play,
In my own jig, I roll away!

The Silent Cipher

Amidst the whispers of my quest,
I scratch my head; I'm not the best.
Each piece a cheeky, silent ghost,
They seem to play, no one I trust.

With a wink and nod, they tease and twirl,
In this grand game, I'm just a girl.
A squiggly bit, a curve or two,
"Are you my match?" I ask—who knew?

A gap so wide, a corner bare,
I laugh aloud, but where's the snare?
With every turn, they dance away,
Teasing me at the end of the day.

The silent cipher won't be solved,
As laughter blooms from this strange world.
So, I'll embrace the mess tonight,
Hum a tune, and fly in flight!

Enigma of Existence

I found a piece that's shaped like cheese,
It winks and giggles, like a tease.
"Do I belong? What a fun ride!"
But without a border, I just slide.

A missing corner, oh what a mess,
The cat thinks it's a toy—no less!
Chasing it round, he pounces and trips,
Life's but a laugh, as chaos flips.

A bright old sun, a cranky cloud,
Laughing together, oh so loud.
"Where do I fit?" I shout in cheer,
But echoes shout, "Nowhere, my dear!"

In this enigma, I snicker and grin,
While the dog steals the show with a silly spin.
So let the pieces roll far and wide,
In this amusing ride, I'll take in stride!

Searching for the Key

In the maze of shapes, I skip and hop,
A mystery door? I can't seem to stop.
With squares and circles on the floor,
I search for a key, could it be more?

A monkey in a hat waves hello,
Offers me clues – or maybe just show.
"Is this a lock?" I ask the air,
The sky chuckles, "Try over there!"

I peek through the cracks, it's quite the sight,
A rainbow of pieces shining bright.
"Which one's the key?" I ponder with cheer,
The pieces giggle, "Not one is near!"

With a wobble dance and bit of flair,
I'll twist and turn without a care.
In searching for keys, I find this bliss,
As laughter unlocks what I thought I'd miss!

Navigating the Unknown

I once lost my keys, what a sight,
They vanished like stars in the night.
I checked under cushions, though they won't show,
The dog thinks it's fun; it's now a game of 'no.'

Maps keep twisting in my confused mind,
Every step forward, another grind.
Around every corner, I still find a mess,
Maybe a treasure? I just can't guess.

With socks that don't match, I walk about,
Who knew chaos could make me shout?
But with laughter and joy, I stumble along,
Perhaps this wild ride is where I belong.

So here's to the journeys where logic has fled,
Embracing the madness, it's fun instead!
Let's toast to the mishaps that make us grin,
When puzzles are jumbled, that's where we win!

Finding Balance in Chaos

Juggling plates while riding a bike,
Who thought balance was something to hype?
Spinning around with a grin so wide,
I'll laugh at the mess, let it be my guide.

Coffee twice spilled on the kitchen floor,
A dance in the mayhem, pulling me more.
With dish soap and laughter, no time to rage,
Who knew that chaos would steal the stage?

Children run wild, a whirlwind of fun,
I try to play referee, but I can't run!
Hugs turn to wrestling, falling like rain,
In this circus of joy, I embrace the strain.

So grab your wild moments, don't let them pass,
In the heart of disorder, let laughter amass.
With a splash and a quirk, let's spin around,
In the dance of the crazy, true joy is found!

The Symphony of the Fragments

A violin string broke; what a tune,
It screeched and wobbled, the cat's in a swoon.
Drums from the cupboard, a disco you see,
Whirling and twirling, a sweet cacophony.

Pots clash with pans in a melodious way,
Who knew cooking could lead to this play?
Chopping the onions leads to a tear,
But with a chorus of chaos, who really cares?

The toaster's a trumpet, the fridge deep with bass,
Rhythm and ruckus fill every place.
We'll dance like wild birds on the edge of the night,
In this crazy concert, everything's right.

So turn up the volume, let laughter ring—
A symphony's chaos can't help but bring.
Together in fragments, we sing and we play,
In the kitchen of life, we'll find our way!

The Fissure of Time

Tick-tock goes the clock, where did it run?
Yesterday's plans blurred almost for fun.
I dashed to the future, fell flat on my face,
In a race with the hours, I need more space.

Coffee cups flying, just seconds to spare,
Who knew that minutes could twist like a hair?
I glance at my watch, it's a sneaky little cheat,
Though somehow it whispers, 'Take a backseat.'

Time's slippery fingers keep pulling me along,
In the rush of the seconds, I learn to be strong.
Hurrying to catch up, I often trip wide,
Yet in slips and slides lies a giggly ride.

Embrace every moment, let laughter burst free,
In the dance with the clock, there's a wild glee.
So bring on the chaos, and let's spin through time,
In a quirky ballet, it'll all be sublime!

Fragments of Existence

In a box rusty and old,
I found bits wrapped in gold.
One looked like a cat's fuzzy tail,
Another, an odd blue whale!

I sift through pieces, a curious task,
Trying to find what I must ask.
Why's my puzzle shaped like a fry?
Is there sauce for that—oh my, oh my!

Some fit snug like a sock on a toe,
While others dance like they just don't know.
I've a corner that looks like a shoe,
But no one will wear it, not even my crew!

With laughter ringing as I try to sort,
Some are there just to torment.
Yet in this chaos, I find delight,
Guess my life's just a jigsaw fight!

Seeking Meaning in Shattered Mirrors

I gaze at glass that's cracked and frayed,
Reflections of me, all mislaid.
One shard shows my hair in a twist,
The other reveals I have no wrist!

In pieces I see a strange new look,
Where my nose is a fish from a book.
My smile is wide, but my chin is lean,
Am I a monster, or just in between?

The whispers of mirrors, they all shout loud,
"Come join our circus, you funky proud!"
I giggle along with the faces I see,
In this kaleidoscope, who could be me?

Chasing laughter through glassy seams,
I gather my thoughts, or maybe just dreams.
In the oddest of fragments, I feel quite fine,
Being a puzzle that's all mine!

The Search for Missing Shapes

I roam through boxes, a treasure hunt,
Looking for shapes, in a bizarre stunt.
Where's the hexagon to match my hat?
Or the triangle to dance with my cat?

Circles are rolling, squares in a plight,
I ponder so deeply, much to my fright.
What's with the piece that looks like a shoe?
Could it be hiding behind the spaghetti? Who knew?

Edges are sharp, the middle's too round,
As I weed through chaos, laughter is found.
I gather my shapes, make a funky crew,
But where's the triangle? It promised to woo!

With giggles and grins, I sort the mess,
Creating a shape-shifting web of success.
In this game of fitting, I shed every fear,
'Cause this puzzle, dear friends, is why I am here!

Where Fitting Pieces Meet

In a world where shapes play hide and seek,
I found pieces of laughter, not weak.
A red one that giggles, a blue that sings,
Twirling together like springtime flings!

Mismatched socks try to form a line,
Arguing 'bout who looks just divine.
But together they learn, when tossed in a pile,
That funky can fit with a jolly old style!

T-shaped and H-shaped, they dance on the floor,
Making new friends as they open new doors.
But when it's time to jump in the game,
Who knew the circle was so very lame?

Yet among all the pieces, there's joy we can find,
In the quirks and the laughs, we're perfectly aligned.
So let's piece together our silly, fun quest,
For in every odd shape, we're truly blessed!

Embracing the Void

In the chaos of socks, a pair disappears,
The dog chews the corner, confirming my fears.
With coffee spills and laughter we stand,
A jigsaw of moments, half-formed and bland.

My t-shirt's inside out, what a style,
My hair's a nest, it's been that way for a while.
Yet joy bubbles up amidst all the mess,
Who needs a corner? I just need to guess!

I search for my keys, they hide with great glee,
A dance with despair, just my cat and me.
In this comedy of errors, we twirl and we spin,
Embracing the chaos, let the laughter begin!

So here's to the void, a place that feels right,
With friends and mischief, it's quite the delight.
We'll toast to our blunders, united we're bold,
In this splendid mayhem, watch stories unfold.

Interwoven Journeys

There's a map in my head, but it's upside down,
Following breadcrumbs, I stumble and frown.
With each twist and turn, I question my way,
Amidst tangled tales, I laugh at the fray.

The cat steals my lunch, and I retaliate,
We play hide and seek, a questionable fate.
Each day's an adventure, like rolling a die,
With ups and with downs, oh how time does fly!

Threads of connections weave through my days,
Like a sock in the dryer, oh how it sways.
A map with no key, yet I wander with glee,
Who needs direction when you're laughing with me?

We'll journey together, through thick and through thin,
In the weave of the fun, let the games begin!
With humor as fuel, we'll burn bright and true,
Interwoven oddities, just me and you.

Casting Light on Shadows

In a room full of junk, the shadows do play,
A dance of the oddities, brightening the gray.
My cat shadow-boxes with ghosts of the night,
While I search for a bright bulb, to shed some more light.

I trip on old memories, they're scattered like dust,
Each one a reminder, in laughter we trust.
Oh, the fridge hums a tune, as I ponder a snack,
With shadows as friends, there's no trace of lack.

I'm casting my doubts onto walls of delight,
As shadows are dancing, I'll join in the fight.
With a flashlight in hand, I'll find every frayed bead,
Turning fumbles and stumbles to whimsical deeds.

So I toast to the shadows, and each little quirk,
In this light-hearted quest, there's magic at work.
With laughter beside me, we're never alone,
In the glow of the moments, I've found my true home.

The Narrative of Gaps

Between eager chapters, the gaps start to show,
A missing puzzle piece? No, just last night's taco!
With hiccups and giggles, my story unfolds,
In the spaces between, laughter's the gold.

With coffee in hand, I ponder the wise,
As cereal dances, and my fingers do spies.
Each gap tells a tale; who needs all the facts?
In the comedy of life, enjoy what subtracts.

There's a place for the awkward, the clumsy, the wild,
Like a kid with a sprout, or a misfit's lost child.
The narrative wobbles, yet joy does entice,
In the gaps of my story, I find paradise.

So here's to the moments that sidestep the flow,
With laughter and fun, we always will grow.
In every shortcoming, there's magic, it seems,
The story's not over—it's bursting with dreams!

www.ingramcontent.com/pod-product-compliance
Lightning Source LLC
Chambersburg PA
CBHW051659160426
43209CB00004B/958